Wood Machine Guide

WITHDRAWN

Terry Bloor
David Wright

Nelson Thornes
a Wolters Kluwer business

Published in 2006 by:
Nelson Thornes Ltd
Delta Place
27 Bath Road
CHELTENHAM
GL53 7TH
United Kingdom

06 07 08 09 10 / 10 9 8 7 6 5 4 3 2 1

A catalogue record for this book is available from the British Library

ISBN 0 7487 9385 2

Photographs by Martin Sookias

Page make-up by Pantek Arts Ltd, Maidstone, Kent

Printed and bound in Croatia by Zrinski

Contents

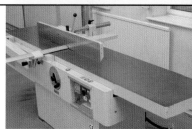

Introduction

This is a step-by-step guide to six wood machines that are commonly used in industry and colleges for NVQ 2 & 3 Wood Occupations. In this guide you will find all the information you need to safely operate these machines to the most current regulations and practices.

Each chapter introduces a different machine and gives you details of the range of work, the parts of the machine, the controls, distancing aids, probable faults and essential maintenance. Each machine is illustrated with full colour photographs to enable you to easily translate the theory into practice.

During your work placement and college training you will probably encounter a range of different wood machines, some of which are covered in this guide and some of which will be slightly different, either because they are made by a different manufacturer or because they are an updated model.

How do you use this guide?

There are a number of features within the guide that are designed to aid your learning; these are,

PUWER '98 boxes: Provision and Use of Work Equipment Regulations 1998 are highlighted, where appropriate, throughout the text.

Questions: There are questions at the end of each chapter to enable you to test your knowledge and identify any weak areas of understanding.

Information: The information section at the back of the guide points you towards resources for further information on each type of machine.

Glossary: The glossary at the back of the guide provides you with a quick and easy definition of wood machinery terms.

Answers to all questions can be found at
www.nelsonthornes.com/courses/carpentryandjoinery

Further Information

Persons using this book should be aware of current legislation applicable to wood working machines and tasks performed on them. Here is a brief description of the laws that affect you; you can find more information at www.hse.gov.uk,

Health & Safety at Work Act 1974 (HASAWA)
These are the main rules that govern health and safety in the workplace. They are there to provide health and safety in the workplace and to protect visitors and members of the public.

Control of Substances Hazardous to Health 2002 (COSHH)
This covers dangerous solids, liquids or gases and gives guidelines on how they should be used and stored. It also gives details of actions the employer and employee must take to protect the health of the individual and others.

Manual Handling Operations Regulations 1992 (amended 2002)
This covers a wide range of manual handling activities including lifting, lowering, pushing, pulling and carrying. It ensures that employers assess and reduce the risk of injury from any hazardous manual handling that can't be avoided.

Noise at Work Regulations 2005
These regulations require employers to prevent or reduce risks to health and safety from exposure to noise at work.

Personal Protective Equipment at Work Regulations 1992 (amended 2002)
These regulations require employers to provide appropriate protective clothing and equipment for their employees, this might include, hard hats, safety footwear, ear defenders, protective gloves, safety goggles etc.

Provision and Use of Work Equipment Regulations 1998 (PUWER)
This regulation requires risks to people's health and safety, from equipment they use at work, to be prevented or controlled. Employers are required to provide equipment that is suitable for the intended use, is safe for use and maintained in a safe condition, is accompanied by suitable safety measures and is only used by people who have received adequate information, instruction and training.

Reporting of Injuries, Diseases and Dangerous Occurrences Regulations 1995 (RIDDOR)
RIDDOR requires employers to report work-related accidents (for example major injuries and deaths or accidents where employees are unable to work for more than three days), diseases and dangerous occurrences to the HSE. This information enables the HSE to identify where and how risks arise and to investigate serious accidents.

Acknowledgements

The authors and publishers gratefully acknowledge the owners of any copyright material reproduced herein. Material reproduced from the HSE and other quotes are © Crown copyright.

The authors and publishers wish to thank the following:

Oldham College for the use of their wood machine workshop for the photographs in this publication.

Wadkin, Griggio and Robinson for allowing us to photograph their machines

Disclaimer

These materials have been developed by Nelson Thornes Ltd and the content and the accuracy are the sole responsibility of Nelson Thornes Ltd. Neither the City and Guilds of London Institute nor the Construction Industry Training Board accept any liability whatsoever in respect of any breach of the intellectual property rights of any third party howsoever occasioned or damage to the third party's property or person as a result of the use of this publication.

Nelson Thornes Ltd take no responsibility for any injuries sustained as a result of following the instructions in this book.

1

Radial Arm Saw

Range of Work

This saw is capable of accurate overhead cross-cutting at 90° and angles of up to 45° in either direction. The saw motor/blade can also be canted over to produce compound cuts. The motor/saw blade is mounted on a carriage that is pulled over the timber-based material to be cut by the operator.

Fig 1.1

Parts of the Machine

Motor/saw blade and table

The motor/saw blade is mounted over a fixed table on a carriage, which in turn is mounted on a column (Fig 1.2). The column has a winding mechanism for the carriage to be vertically adjusted; the carriage also pivots on the column to 45° to the left or right. The motor/saw blade travels horizontally on the carriage. The table has a slot to accommodate the tips of the blade during the machining process.

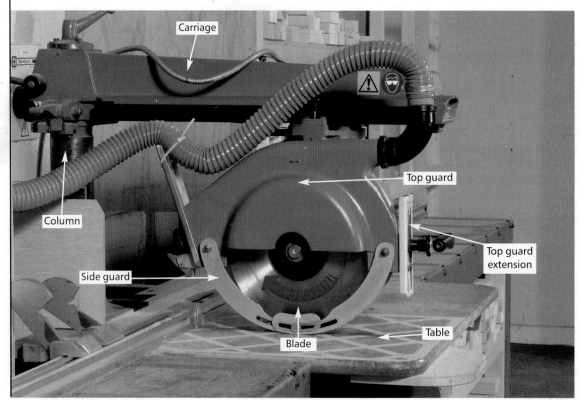

Fig 1.2

Top guard

This is made from aluminium. Its function is to guard the top portion of the saw blade to prevent accidental contact with it. In all cases the saw blade must be guarded and have flanges on both sides of the guard (Fig 1.2).

Side guards

These are made from steel. Their function is to guard the teeth of the saw blade. The guards rely on gravity to remain set correctly (Fig 1.2).

Top guard extension

This is made from steel. Its function is to guard the saw blade between the timber based material and top guard (Fig 1.3).

> The guard must be adjusted as close to the work-piece as possible.

Fig 1.3

Spring assisted return wire

This is installed to ensure that the saw unit returns to its safe rest position when released (Fig 1.4).

Fig 1.4

Fig 1.5

Fence

The fence is made from aluminium, runs the full length of the machine and is square to the saw blade (Figs 1.5 and 1.6).

Gauge and adjustable stops

The gauge has measurements clearly displayed along the full length of the fence with adjustable steel stops for accurate cutting of timber-based material (Figs 1.5 and 1.6).

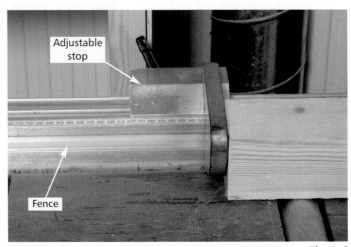

Fig 1.6

Roller tables

These are positioned on either side of the table to support and allow easy positioning of the timber-based material to be cut (Fig 1.7).

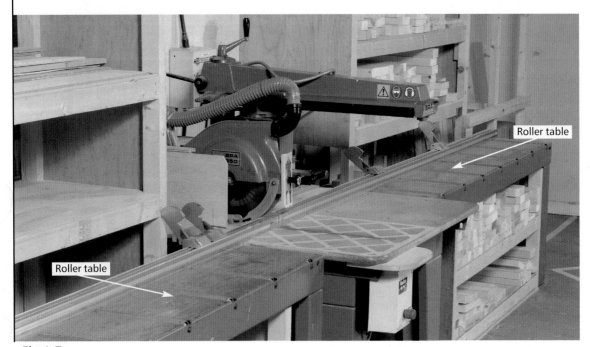

Fig 1.7

Square cross-cutting

The motor/blade can be set at 90° to the fence and table for square cross-cutting (Fig 1.8).

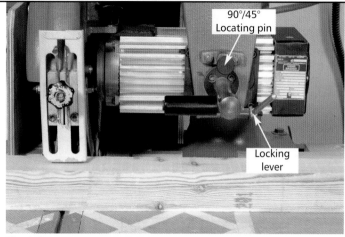

Fig 1.8

Jigs

Jigs are made by the machinist to enable certain operational cuts to be carried out safely. They must be of substantial construction, be safe to use and not endanger the operative using the jig.

Mitring

The motor/blade can be set at 90° to the table and at any angle up to 45° to the fence for mitring. (Fig 1.9). A jig comprising a fence and bed is used to prevent the fixed fence from becoming damaged.

Fig 1.9

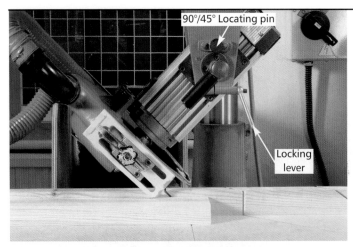

The motor/blade can be set at 90° to the fence and at any angle from 90° to 0° to the table for mitring (Fig 1.10).

A combination of angles to fence and table can be used to produce a compound mitre (Fig 1.11).

Fig 1.10

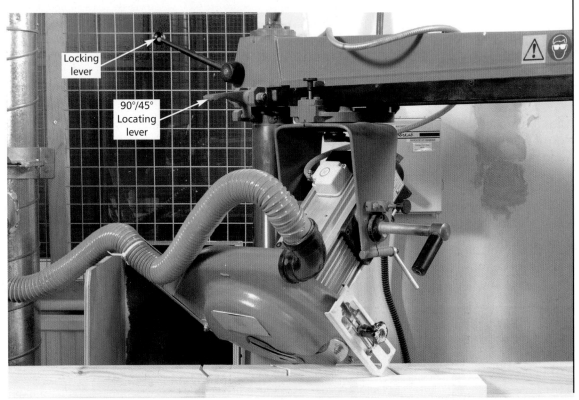

Fig 1.11

Controls

Stop/start buttons, brake

These buttons must operate efficiently and be within easy reach of the operator. The stop button has a 'mushroom head' and a twist-to-release mechanism. The start button is shrouded to prevent accidental starting (Fig 1.12). To reduce the risk of contact with the saw blade during 'run down', machines should be fitted with a braking device. The braking device is automatic and works in conjunction with the stop button.

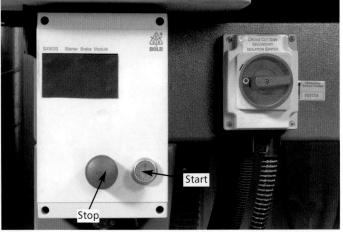

Fig 1.12

Isolator

Its function is to cut off all power to the machine when setting up, changing tooling or carrying out repairs. The isolator should also be used when the machine is left unattended.

There are two isolators for this machine. One is on the wall behind the machine (Fig 1.13). This is used when work is completed, as it is easy to see that the machine is isolated. The other is situated by the start switch (Fig 1.14) and is easier to use when adjusting/replacing tooling. Both can be locked 'off' using a padlock.

Fig 1.13

Fig 1.14

Distancing aids

A push stick should always be used when inadequate space is available to hold the material securely by hand. Hands should never be closer than is necessary to the front of the saw blade, and they should never be in line with the blade. A push stick or spike should be used to remove small pieces from the area of the saw blade.

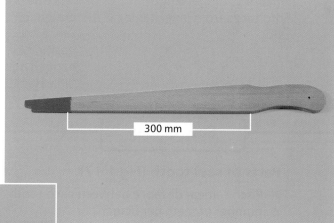

Fig 1.15 Push stick

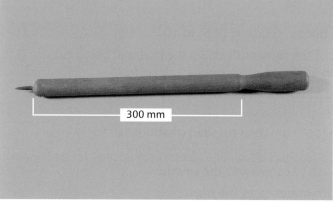

Fig 1.16 Spike

Fault diagnosis

Table 1.1 lists the more common faults, which may occur when cross-cutting timber-based products.

Table 1.1

Fault	Possible cause	Remedy
Cutting out of square horizontally	▶ Misalignment of carriage	▶ Re-align carriage (square to fence)
Cutting out of square vertically	▶ Misalignment of saw blade/motor	▶ Re-align saw blade/motor (square to table)
Saw tends to 'bite' into the timber	▶ Dull saw blade ▶ Ripping blade being used for cross-cutting ▶ Twisted/badly seasoned timber causing kerf to close on to the blade ▶ Incorrectly orientated timber	▶ Replace blade with the correct type ▶ Cut gradually, easing back and re-cutting as binding occurs ▶ Re-orientate timber
Saw wobbles badly	▶ Loss of tension. Loose nut. Overheating due to abrasive timber dulling teeth. Insufficient set	▶ Re-tension saw blade (specialist job). Re-tighten nut. Re-sharpen/re-set saw
Saw slows down when cutting	▶ Dull saw blade. Resin build-up on teeth	▶ Re-sharpen saw blade. Clean blade
Incorrect timber length produced from 'adjustable stop'	▶ Fence incorrectly positioned ▶ Fence knocked out of position by timber being banged against 'adjustable stops'	▶ Re-position fence

Saw blades

Parts of saw tooth (Fig 1.17)

▶ *Pitch* – linear distance between each tooth. The pitch determines the gullet size and number of teeth per blade.

▶ *Hook* – For cross-cutting a negative hook is required of 5° to 10°

▶ *Clearance angle* – ensures the heel of the saw tooth clears the material being cut (softwoods 15° and hardwoods 5° to 15°).

▶ *Top bevel* – the angle across the top of the tooth (softwoods 15° and hardwoods 5° to 10°).

▶ *Front bevel* – across the face of the tooth (nil for a rip saw) of about 10° for cross-cutting.

▶ *Gullet* – the space between each tooth to carry away the sawdust.

▶ *Back of the tooth* – edge of the tooth opposite to the front.

▶ *Root* – base of the tooth.

▶ *Face of the tooth* – leading edge of the tooth.

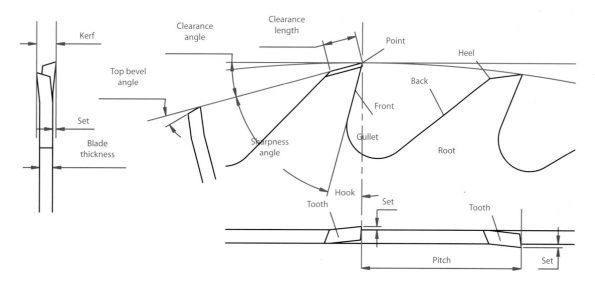

Fig 1.17

▶ **Set** – amount each tooth is offset to give clearance to the saw plate.

▶ **Saw kerf** – blade thickness plus twice the set on the saw = total width of cut made by the saw blade.

Maintenance

Tungsten carbide tipped saw blades

When cutting abrasive timbers or any sheet materials, tungsten carbide tipped (TCT) saw blades should be used because they stay sharp longer. These saw blades will also have a 'negative' hook (Fig 1.18). The tips will also have a specific shape depending upon use.

Fig 1.18

Cleaning off resin deposits

There are several systems for cleaning off resin deposits, which use a tank or tray with a resin solvent, that do the job effectively. However, the most common method is the use of paraffin or white spirit. Brushed on then scraped off with a scraper made from timber. Do not forget to clean out the gullets.

Examining the saw teeth for cracks

Cracks, when they occur are usually in the gullet area, in line with the face of the tooth. These are generally the result of incorrect filing giving a sharp corner in the gullet, or overheating at the base of the gullet when using a grinding wheel for gulleting.

Cracks are not always obvious to the naked eye and the procedure is to ring the saw and listen to the sound. If it is suspect, a further test is to apply paraffin, wipe off the surplus with a rag, then apply French chalk powder over the saw plate. Leave for a period, wipe off the chalk, then a black line highlighting the crack should be visible.

Storage of the saw blades

The saw blades may be stored on a peg with a plywood spacer between each to prevent damage to teeth (Fig 1.19).

Fig 1.19

Questions

1. What tasks can be carried out on the radial arm saw?

    . . . .

    . . . .

    . . . .

    . . . .

    . . . .

2. What regulations cover the construction, setting up and using of the radial arm saw?

    . . . .

    . . . .

    . . . .

    . . . .

    . . . .

3. Which is the correct blade to use when cross-cutting timber on the radial arm saw?

    . . . .

    . . . .

    . . . .

Questions

4. What is the maximum time allowed for the brake to stop the rotation of the blade?

. . . .

. . . .

. . . .

5. What is the name given to the guard fitted above the saw blade?

. . . .

. . . .

. . . .

6. How close to the material being cut should the guard(s) be positioned?

. . . .

. . . .

. . . .

7. Before adjusting any part of the machine what must be done?

. . . .

. . . .

. . . .

. . . .

. . . .

. . . .

8. How should circular saw blades be stored and why?

. . . .

. . . .

. . . .

. . . .

. . . .

. . . .

9. What is the purpose of the side guards and how are they set?

. . . .

. . . .

. . . .

. . . .

. . . .

. . . .

Questions

10. Why is it necessary to have a return mechanism on the saw carriage?

. . . .

. . . .

. . . .

. . . .

. . . .

2

Dimension Saw

Range of work

Fig 2.1

This is a versatile circular saw. It is capable of accurate sawing, both with and across the grain (depending on the type of blade fitted). The saw blade itself can be canted, enabling bevel cutting to be carried out. It can also be raised and lowered. The sliding table to the left of the blade allows for accurate cutting of sheet materials, square, angle and compound cuts of wood based products. The dimension saw is designed for precision work, and is not suitable for high levels of production for the following reasons:

▶ Push bench, i.e. it is handfed, which limits the level of production possible (compared with power feed)

▶ Use of heavier gauge saw blades, increases amount of waste (sawdust) and increases feed resistance

▶ The maximum saw diameter (450 mm) limits the depth of cut.

Parts of the machine

Table

The table is made from cast iron with a ground surface. One half (to the right of the blade) is fixed. The 'other half' moves on rollers for cross-cutting, bevel and compound cutting (Fig 2.2). It can also be locked in position for ripping. Slide locks are released to allow this table to slide out sideways for access for saw blade/riving knife changing.

Fig 2.2

Riving knife

This is made from spring tempered steel. Its function is to:

▶ Prevent timber binding on the saw after cutting

▶ Act as a guard to the up running part of the saw blade (Fig 2.3).

The riving knife must be fixed securely below the machine table and be adjusted so that it is in line with the blade, and follows the sweep of the saw blade, as the blade has a vertical adjustment.

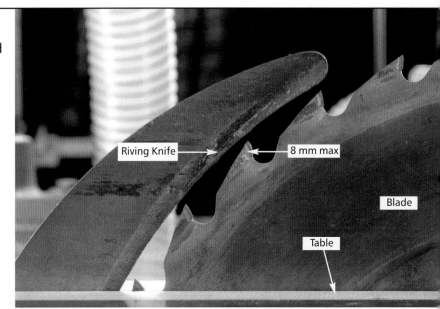

Fig 2.3

The maximum distance between the riving knife and the saw blade at table level is 8 mm.

The thickness of the riving knife should be thicker than the plate of the saw but thinner than the width of cut (Kerf).

The height of the riving knife should be kept adjusted so the vertical distance between the top of the blade and the riving knife is no more than 25 mm, except for saw blades that are more than 600 mm in diameter; in which case the top of the riving knife should be to a height of at least 225 mm above the machine table.

Crown guard

The crown guard is made from steel/aluminium. Its function is to guard the top portion of the saw blade to prevent accidental contact with it. In all cases the saw blade must be guarded and have flanges on both sides.

The guard must be adjusted as close to the workpiece as possible (Fig 2.4).

Fig 2.4

Extension piece

This is made from steel. Its function is to guard the saw blade between the workpiece and the crown guard when cutting narrow pieces of material, when the crown guard cannot be lowered sufficiently, due to its fouling on the fence.

> The extension piece should be set as close as possible to the surface of the workpiece.

Fig 2.5

Saw fence

The function of the saw fence is to act as a guide to the timber, to ensure a parallel cut (Fig 2.6).

It can also be canted up to 45° for bevel cuts (Fig 2.7).

Fig 2.6

Fig 2.7

Fig 2.8

It can be adjusted fore and aft to suit the diameter of the saw being used. The end of the fence should be in line with the bottom of the gullets at table level (Fig 2.8).

Setscrews at the back of the fence can be adjusted to give the fence 'lead in' or 'lead out' to obtain a parallel cut with different blades. Insufficient 'lead out' or 'off set' is a common cause of 'black eyes' on the blade. As a guide the 'lead out' should be 3 mm in 6000 mm of length. Therefore, the 'lead out' on a 600 mm diameter saw blade should be 0.3 mm.

Fine adjustment for saw fence

Fine adjustment on the saw fence gives correct width and thickness without completely unlocking or moving the fence manually (Fig 2.9)

Fig 2.9

Angle fence

It is fitted to the sliding table to the left of the saw blade. It can be set at right angles to the saw blade giving accurate cross-cutting of materials at 90°, or set at any required angle to give a bevelled cut (Fig 2.10). The saw blade can also be canted over and the fence set at the required angle to give a compound bevelled cut.

Fig 2.10

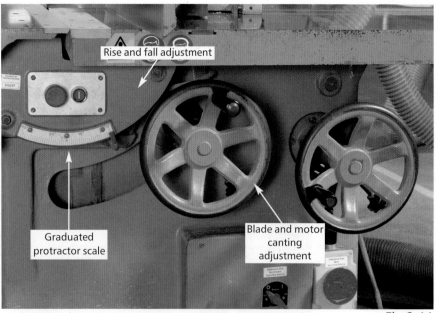

Graduated protractor scale

Rise and fall adjustment

Blade and motor canting adjustment

Fig 2.11

Rise and fall mechanism

A hand wheel is turned to raise or lower the saw spindle/riving knife. For ideal sawing, the roots of the teeth should project just above the surface of the material being cut. This allows more efficient guarding of the blade and a smoother cut with less 'breakout' on the underside of the material (Fig 2.11).

Blade and motor canting

The saw blade and motor can be canted over from the vertical to an angle of 45°. A graduated protractor scale indicates the angle (Fig 2.11).

Blade size and adjustment

Minimum diameters of saw blades

The diameter of the smallest saw blade that can be safely used should be marked clearly on the machine. A small diameter blade (less than 60 per cent or 6/10 of the largest blade the saw can accommodate) will have reduced peripheral blade speed and will reduce efficiency, cause jamming and produce excessive loads on both blade and motor.

Example
Maximum size of blade 650 mm
Minimum diameter = $650 \times 6/10$
Allowed = 390 mm diameter.

Extension table

An extension table is required behind the saw if an assistant is employed at the outfeed end to remove cut pieces.

The assistant should always stand behind the extension table when 'pulling off' (Fig 2.12).

The table should be extended so that the distance between the saw blade spindle and the rear edge of the table is at least 1200 mm in length and the width of the saw table.

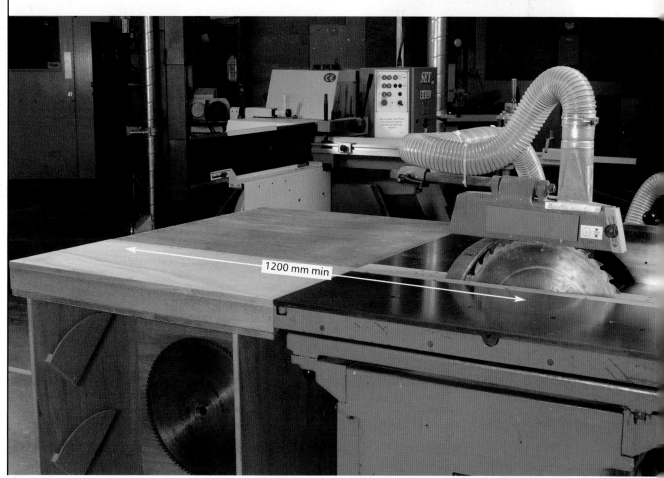

1200 mm min

Fig 2.12

Flatting and deeping

The dimension saw can be used as a conventional rip saw for flatting (Fig 2.13) and deeping (Fig 2.14). However the blade diameter restricts these operations.

Fig 2.13

Fig 2.14

Square cross-cutting and mitring

The dimension saw can be used for square cross-cutting (Fig 2.15) and mitring (Fig 2.16).

Fig 2.15

Fig 2.16

Controls

Stop/start buttons, brake

All buttons must operate efficiently and be within easy reach of the operator. The stop button has a 'mushroom head' and a 'pull to release' mechanism. The start button is shrouded to prevent accidental starting (Fig 2.17). This is to reduce the risk of contact with the saw blade during 'run down'. The braking device is manually operated (Fig 2.18) and also actuates the stop button. However, it does not put the stop button in the locked position.

Fig 2.17

Machines should be fitted with a braking device that brings the blade to rest within 10 seconds.

Fig 2.18

Isolator

The function of the isolator is to cut off all power to the machine when setting up, changing tooling or carrying out repairs, and should also be used when the machine is left unattended (Fig 2.19).

Fig 2.19

Distancing aids

The leading hand should never be closer than is necessary to the front of the saw blade, and hands should never be in line with the blade.

A push stick or spike should be used to remove the cut piece from between the saw blade and fence. A push block should be used to control short pieces of timber (normally expensive hardwoods) when converting to required dimensions.

> A push stick should always be used when making any cut of less than 300 mm in length, or when feeding the last 300 mm of a longer cut.

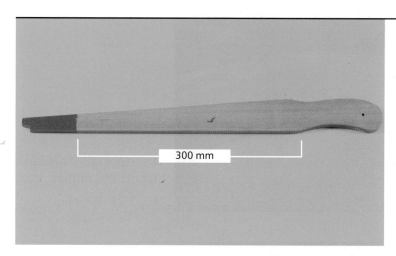

Fig 2.20 Push stick

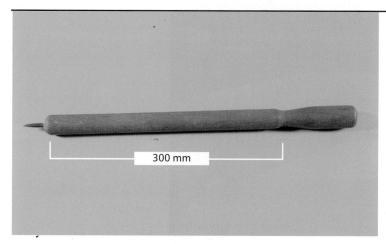

Fig 2.21 Spike

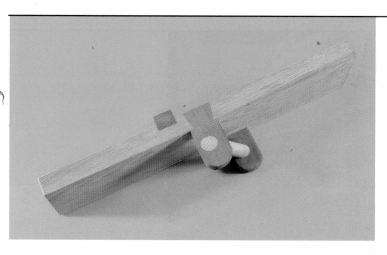

Fig 2.22 Push block

Jigs

Jigs are made by the machinist to enable certain operational cuts to be carried out safely. They must be of substantial construction be safe to use and not endanger the operative using the jig

For cutting triangular lengths of timber

Fig 2.23 Fillet jig

90°

For cutting bevelled lengths of timber

Fig 2.24 Bevel jig

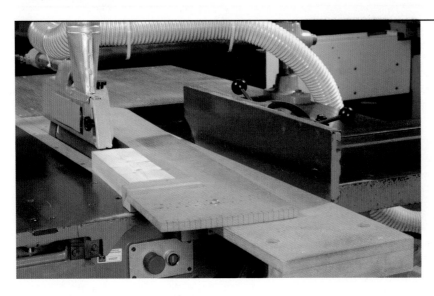

For cutting tapered lengths of timber

Fig 2.25 Taper jig

Fault diagnosis

Table 2.1 lists the more common faults that may occur when ripping timber-based products.

Fault	Possible cause	Remedy
Work moves away from fence	Misalignment of fence – too much 'lead in'	▶ Re-align fence
Work moves towards the side of the saw causing friction and binding	▶ Too much lead in	▶ Re-align fence
Work pulls to one side or other of saw	▶ Saw teeth longer one side than the other. Saw teeth set greater on one side	▶ Stone the saw, set evenly and re-sharpen (specialist job)
Saw tends to lift the timber and throw the piece back	▶ Dull saw blade. Cross-cut blade being used for ripping. Wood binding on the blade due to insufficient clearance. Twisted/badly seasoned timber causing kerf to close on to the blade	▶ Replace blade with the correct type. Feed timber in gradually, easing back as binding occurs
Saw wobbles badly	▶ Loss of tension. Loose nut. Overheating due to abrasive timber dulling teeth. Insufficient set	▶ Re-tension saw blade (specialist job). Re-tighten nut. Re-sharpen/re-set saw
Saw slows down when cutting	▶ Belts too slack on pulleys. Dull saw blade. Resin build-up on teeth	▶ Re-tension belts. Re-sharpen saw blade. Clean blade
Timber sticking	▶ Resin on saw blade	▶ Stop machine. Remove blade, clean and replace

Saw blades

Held securely in place on the spindle with a washer and nut, the thread on the spindle and nut are oriented to ensure the nut tightens as the machine starts (nut tightens in the opposite direction to the rotation of the blade).

Parts of saw tooth

▶ *Pitch* – linear distance between each tooth. The pitch determines the gullet size and number of teeth per blade.

▶ *Hook* – For ripping a positive hook is required. Hardwoods require 10° to 15° with a maximum of 20°; softwoods 25° with a maximum of 30° (Fig 2.27). For cross-cutting a negative hook is required of 5° to 10° (Fig 2.26).

▶ **Clearance angle** – to ensure the heel of the saw tooth clears the material being cut (softwoods 15° and hardwoods 5° to 15°).

▶ **Top bevel** – the angle across the top of the tooth (softwoods 15° and hardwoods 5° to 10°).

▶ **Front bevel** – across the face of the tooth (nil for a rip saw) of about 10° for cross-cutting.

▶ **Gullet** – space between each tooth to carry away the saw dust.

▶ **Back of the tooth** – edge of the tooth opposite to the front.

▶ **Root** – base of the tooth.

▶ **Face of the tooth** – leading edge of the tooth.

▶ **Set** – amount each tooth is off-set to give clearance to the saw plate.

▶ **Saw kerf** – blade thickness plus twice the set on the saw = total width of cut made by the saw blade.

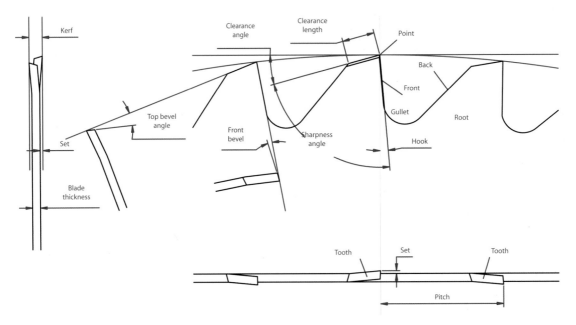

Fig 2.26

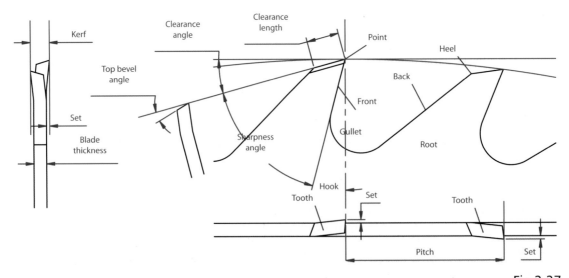

Fig 2.27

Tungsten carbide tipped saw blades

When cutting abrasive timbers or any sheet materials, tungsten carbide tipped (TCT) saw blades should be used because they stay sharp longer. These saw blades will also have a 'negative' (Fig 2.28) or 'positive' (Fig 2.29) hook, The tips will also have a specific shape depending upon use.

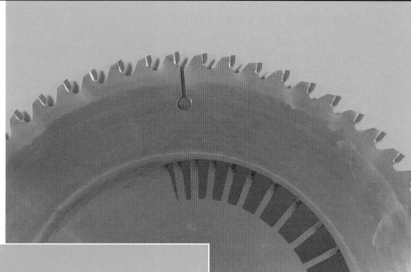

Fig 2.28

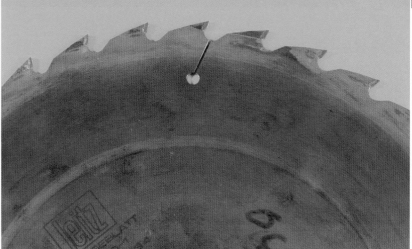

Fig 2.29

Maintenance

Cleaning off resin deposits

There are several systems for cleaning of resin deposits, which use a tank or tray with a resin solvent that does the job effectively. However, the most common method is the use of paraffin or white spirit. Brushed on, then scraped off with a scraper made from timber. Do not forget to clean out the gullets.

Examining the saw teeth for cracks

Cracks, when they occur are usually in the gullet area, in line with the face of the tooth and are generally the result of incorrect filing giving a sharp corner in the gullet, or overheating at the base of the gullet when using a grinding wheel for gulleting.

Cracks are not always obvious to the naked eye and the procedure is to ring the saw and listen to the sound. If this is suspect, a further test is to apply paraffin, wipe off the surplus with a rag, then apply French chalk powder over the saw plate. Leave for a period, wipe off the chalk, then a black line highlighting the crack should be visible.

Storage of the saw blades

Where the saw blade is being removed from the machine, to be replaced by a different blade, the riving knife may/will require changing to match the 'new' saw blade being fitted.

The saw blades may be stored on a peg with a plywood spacer between each to prevent damage to teeth (Fig 2.30).

Riving knives should be clearly marked regarding which saw blade they belong to (Fig 2.31).

Fig 2.30

Fig 2.31

Questions

1. What tasks can be carried out on the dimension saw?

    . . . .

    . . . .

    . . . .

    . . . .

    . . . .

    . . . .

2. What regulations cover the construction, setting up and using of the dimension saw?

    . . . .

    . . . .

Questions

. . . .

. . . .

. . . .

. . . .

. . . .

3. Which is the correct blade to use when ripping a piece of abrasive timber?

. . . .

. . . .

. . . .

4. What determines the minimum diameter of blade which can be fitted to the saw table?

. . . .

. . . .

. . . .

. . . .

5. State why a riving knife is positioned at the rear or the up running part of the saw blade?

. . . .

. . . .

. . . .

. . . .

6. State the thickness of the riving knife in relation to the blade?

. . . .

. . . .

. . . .

7. What is the maximum distance allowed between the front edge of the riving knife and the saw blade (at table height)?

. . . .

. . . .

. . . .

8. What is the maximum time allowed for the brake to stop the rotation of the blade?

. . . .

. . . .

. . . .

Questions

9. What is the name given to the guard fitted above the saw blade?

   ....

   ....

   ....

10. How close to the material being cut should the guard(s) be positioned?

    ....

    ....

    ....

11. At table height, where should the front edge of the fence be in relation to the saw blade?

    ....

    ....

    ....

    ....

12. What is a push stick and when should it be used?

    ....

    ....

    ....

    ....

    ....

    ....

3

Surface Planer

Range of work

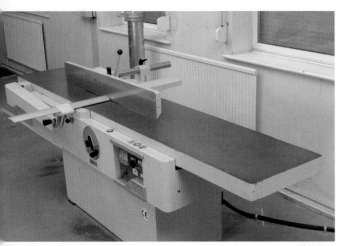

For straightening timber on one face and one side; it is important that the first face and edge are square to one another as this influences the accuracy of subsequent machining operations. Chamfering can also be carried out, but the 'Shaw Guard' must be in position and correctly adjusted.

Fig 3.1

Parts of the machine

Tables

There are two precision ground tables which can be adjusted to suit the cutter knives (Fig 3.2).

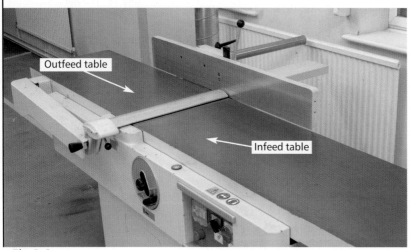

Outfeed table

Infeed table

The outfeed table is set so that its surface is in line with the cutting circle of the block (Fig 3.3). The outfeed table height should never be below the cutting circle diameter.

Fig 3.2

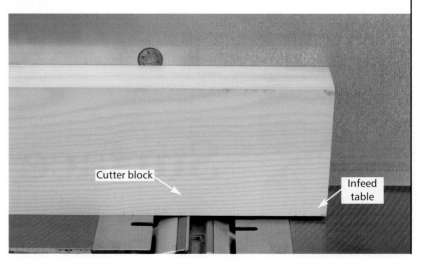

Cutter block

Infeed table

Fig 3.3

The depth of cut is set by adjusting the infeed table by the required amount (Fig 3.4). This is between 1.5 mm to 2 mm for 'straight' sawn timber and increases up to 3 mm for planing up bowed timber.

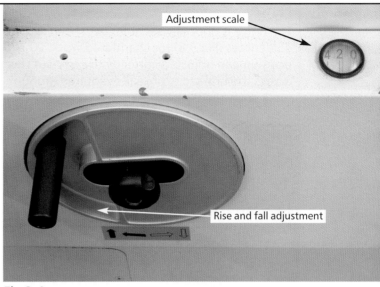

Fig 3.4

Noise reduction

Both table lips have a series of slots machined into them. This is to reduce air buffeting, therefore reducing the noise produced (Fig 3.5).

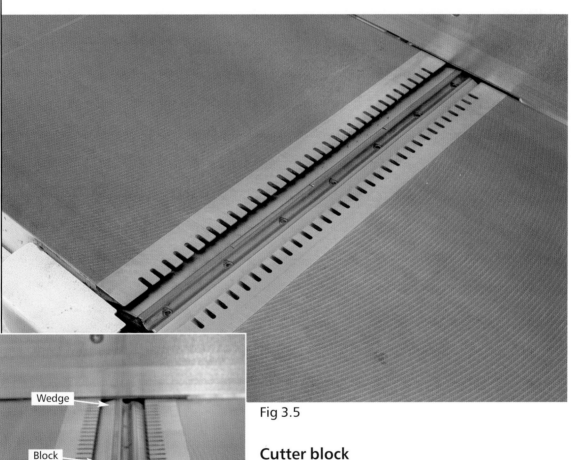

Fig 3.5

Cutter block

This machine is fitted with a 'tersa' block and has reversible/disposable cutters (Fig 3.6). The projection of the cutters is set at 1 mm. The clearance between the cutting circle and the lips of the infeed/outfeed tables should be as close as possible (generally 3 mm + or × 2 mm).

Fig 3.6

Only a cylindrical (or 'round form') cutter block should be used on hand-fed planing machines.

The maximum cutter projection for a round form tool is 3 mm.

Fence

The fence is normally set at 90 degrees (Fig 3.7), but can be canted over to 45 degrees (Fig 3.8) for chamfered work. (The 'Shaw guard' should be in position and adjusted correctly to carry out this task.) It can be adjusted across the table to expose the required amount of blade to carry out the work envisaged.

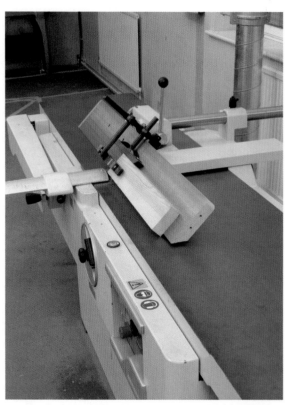

Fig 3.7

Fig 3.8

Bridge guard

This is made from aluminium. It must be strong, ridged, easily adjusted and centrally mounted over the cutter block (Fig 3.9).

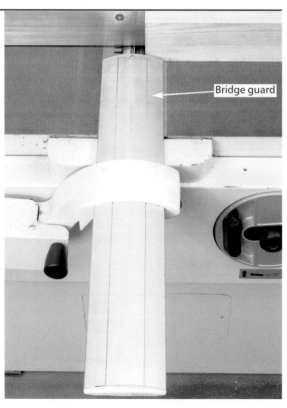

Bridge guard

Fig 3.9

Facing and edging

The bridge guard must be adjusted to give the maximum degree of protection against coming into contact with the rotating cutters. It must be adjusted as shown in Figs 3.10 to 3.13 before making trial cuts.

Fig 3.10 Adjustment of bridge guard for facing

Fig 3.11 Adjustment of bridge guard for edging

Fig 3.12 Adjustment of the bridge guard for flatting and edging, showing flatting

Fig 3.13 Adjustment of the bridge guard for flatting and edging, showing edging

Controls

Controls must operate effectively and be within easy reach of the operator. The stop button must have a 'mushroom head' and a pull or twist release
   A four position switch is situated on the side of the machine and is operated as follows:

Machines must be fitted with a braking device that brings the blade to rest within 10 seconds.

Switch off position (Fig 3.14) activates brake. It is fitted with a braked motor, that does not require power for the brake to operate (isolator off and main stop switch in).

First start position (Fig 3.15). The motor must reach full speed before switching any further (isolator on and main stop switch out).

Fig 3.14

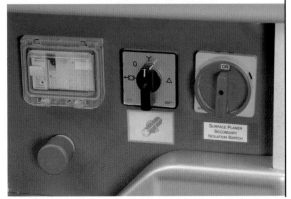

Fig 3.15

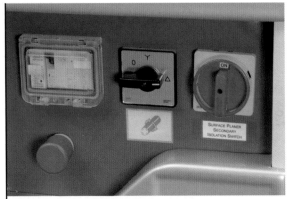

Fig 3.16

Fig 3.17

Second speed position (Fig 3.16) activates the top speed of the cutter block (isolator on and main stop switch out).

Brake release (Fig 3.17) requires power to operate and releases brake approximately 12 seconds after activation (isolator on and main stop switch in).

Isolator

Its function is to cut off all power to the machine when setting up, changing tooling or carrying out repairs. It should also be used when the machine is left unattended. There are two for this machine, one is on the wall behind the machine (Fig 3.18); this is used when work is completed. It is easy to see that the machine is isolated.

The other is situated by the start switch (Fig 3.19). It is easier to use when adjusting or replacing knives. Both can be locked 'off' using a padlock.

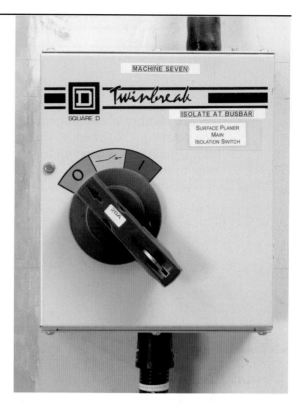

Fig 3.18

Fig 3.19

Distancing aids

Push block

This is used as a purpose-made 'distancing aid' to control short pieces of timber whilst planing up face side (Fig 3.20) or edge. The bridge guard is adjusted up to the edge of the push block.

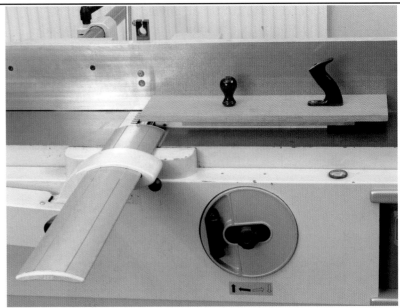

Fig 3.20

Fault diagnosis

Table 3.1 lists the more common faults that may occur when planing up the face side and face edge on timber.

Table 3.1

Fault	Cause	Remedy
The timber rocks and the edge is rounded in length after being surfaced	▶ Outfeed table is set too high above the cutting circle ▶ Table is out of alignment with the cutters ▶ Chippings lie between timber and table ▶ The timber is placed round edge down	▶ Re-adjust outfeed table ▶ Check for wear or maladjustment of slides on the tables ▶ Clear chippings ▶ Place timber hollow edge down
Uneven finish	▶ Dull cutters causing 'chatter' marks on timber ▶ An uneven feed rate	▶ Reverse/replace cutters ▶ Feed timber into cutters at the correct rate
Pronounced cuttermark pattern	▶ Too fast feed rate	▶ Reduce feed rate
Timber 'drops' at the end of cut and gouges out end of the timber	▶ Outfeed table is too low	▶ Adjust the outfeed table level with cutting circle
Excessive vibration causing a poor finish	▶ Worn bearings	▶ Renew bearings
Edge of timber is not square to face	▶ Fence out of square with table	▶ Adjust fence square to table

Maintenance

Planer knife storage

This is supplied in a protective packaging and should remain so until required.

Planer knife disposal

Planer knives should be wrapped in protective packaging and disposed of correctly (they are still dangerous even though they are blunt!).

Questions

1. What tasks can be carried out on the surface planer?

   ....

   ....

   ....

   ....

   ....

   ....

2. Where should the bridge guard be positioned in relation to the material being planed?

   ....

   ....

   ....

   ....

3. Slots are machined in the infeed and outfeed tables either side of the cutter block for what purpose?

   ....

   ....

   ....

   ....

   ....

   ....

4. The depth of cut is controlled by the positioning of which table?

   ....

   ....

   ....

   ....

5. In relation to the cutting circle, where should the outfeed table be positioned?

    . . . .

    . . . .

    . . . .

    . . . .

6. State the maximum projection of blade in a cylindrical cutter block?

    . . . .

    . . . .

    . . . .

    . . . .

7. What would be the cause of pitch marks exceeding 2.5 mm on a piece of material that has been planed?

    . . . .

    . . . .

    . . . .

    . . . .

    . . . .

    . . . .

8. What is the maximum time allowed for the brake to stop the rotation of the cutter block?

    . . . .

    . . . .

    . . . .

    . . . .

9. Which is the correct guard to use when chamfering?

    . . . .

    . . . .

    . . . .

    . . . .

    . . . .

    . . . .

10. What is the purpose of a 'push block' when planing short lengths of timber?

. . . .

. . . .

. . . .

. . . .

. . . .

. . . .

. . . .

11. When replacing the cutter blades what precaution should be taken?

. . . .

. . . .

. . . .

. . . .

. . . .

. . . .

. . . .

12. What do the regulations state that authorised users should be?

. . . .

. . . .

. . . .

. . . .

. . . .

. . . .

4

Combination Planer

Range of work

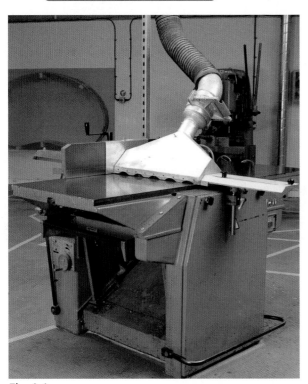

Fig 4.1

Function 1

The function is to straighten timber on one face and one side, in preparation for bringing it to a specified size on the thickness planer. It is important that the first face and edge are square to one another as this influences the accuracy of subsequent machining operations. Bevelling/chamfering can also be carried out. A Shaw guard must be used when carrying out this operation.

Parts of the machine

Tables

There are two precision ground tables that can be adjusted to suit the cutter knives. The outfeed table is set so that its surface is in line with the cutting circle of the block (the out-feed table height should never be below the cutting circle diameter). The depth of cut is set by adjusting the infeed table by the required amount. (between 1.5 mm to 2 mm for 'straight' sawn timber, increased up to 3 mm for planing up bowed timber) (Fig 4.2).

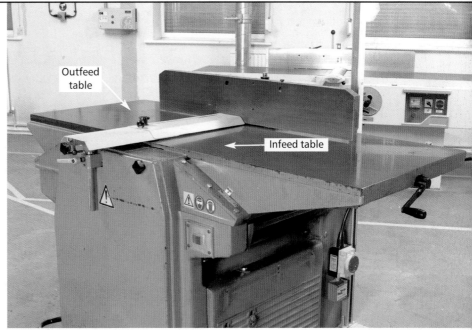

Outfeed table

Infeed table

Fig 4.2

The outfeed table is set so that its surface is in line with the cutting circle of the block (Fig 4.3). The outfeed table height should never be below the cutting circle diameter.

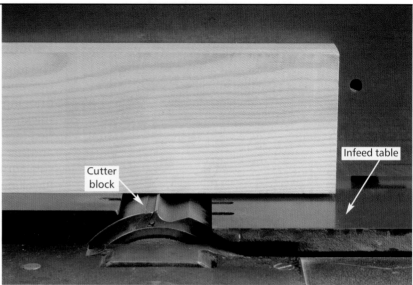

Fig 4.3

The depth of cut is set by adjusting the infeed table by the required amount (Fig 4.4). This should be between 1.5 mm to 2 mm for 'straight' sawn timber, increasing up to 3 mm for planing up bowed timber.

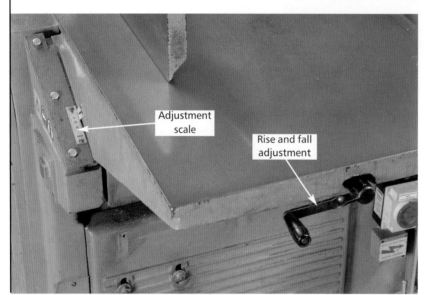

Fig 4.4

Noise reduction

Both table lips have a series of slots machined into them, this is to reduce air buffeting, therefore reducing the noise produced (Fig 4.5).

Fig 4.5

Cutter block

This machine is fitted with a 'tersa' block and has reversible/disposable cutters (Fig 4.6). The projection of the cutters is set at 1 mm. The clearance between the cutting circle and the lips of the infeed/outfeed tables should be as close as possible, generally 3 mm + or –2 mm.

Only a cylindrical (or 'round form') cutter block should be used on hand-fed planing machines.

The maximum projection for a round form tool is 3 mm.

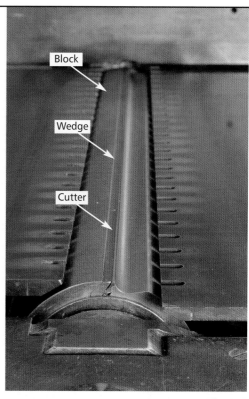

Block

Wedge

Cutter

Fig 4.6

Fence

The fence is normally set at 90° (Fig 4.7), but it can be canted over to 45° (Fig 4.8) for chamfered work. (The 'saw guard' should be in position and adjusted correctly to carry out this task.) It can be adjusted across the table to expose the required amount of blade to carry out the work envisaged.

Fig 4.7

Fig 4.8

Bridge guard

This is made from steel. It must be strong, ridged, easily adjusted and centrally mounted over the cutter block (Fig 4.9).

The bridge guard must be adjusted as close to the workpiece as possible.

Fig 4.9

Facing and edging

The planer must be adjusted to give the maximum degree of protection against coming into contact with the rotating cutters. It must be adjusted as shown in Figs 4.10 to 4.13 before making trial cuts.

Fig 4.10 Adjustment of bridge guard for facing

Fig 4.11 Adjustment of bridge guard for edging

Fig 4.12 Adjustment of bridge guard for facing and edging, showing facing

Fig 4.13 Adjustment of bridge guard for facing and edging, showing edging

Controls

Stop/start switch, brake

These must operate efficiently and be within easy reach of the operator. The stop button must be raised. The start button is recessed to prevent accidental starting. To reduce the risk of contact with the knives during 'run down', machines must be fitted with a braking device. The braking device is manually operated and also acts as a stop switch (Fig 4.14).

> Machines must be fitted with a braking device that brings the blade to rest within 10 seconds.

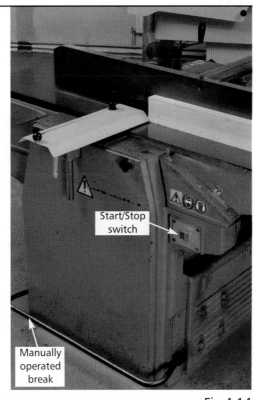

Start/Stop switch

Manually operated break

Fig 4.14

Isolator

The function of the isolator is to cut of all power to the machine when setting up, changing tooling or carrying out repairs. It should also be used when the machine is left unattended. It can be locked 'off' using a padlock (Fig 4.15).

Fig 4.15

Distancing aids

Push block

This is used as a 'distancing aid' to control short pieces of timber whilst planing up the face side/edge. The bridge guard is adjusted up to the edge of the push block (Fig 4.16).

Fig 4.16

Fault diagnosis

Table 4.1 lists the more common faults that may occur when planing up the face side and face edge on timber.

Table 4.1

Fault	Cause	Remedy
Timber hits the front edge of outfeed table	▶ Outfeed table is set too high above the cutting circle	▶ Re-adjust outfeed table
Timber rocks, edge is rounded in length after being surfaced	▶ Outfeed table is set too high above the cutting circle ▶ Table is out of alignment with the cutters ▶ Chippings lie between timber and table ▶ The timber is placed 'round face' down	▶ Re-adjust outfeed table ▶ Check for wear or maladjustment of slides on the tables ▶ Clear chippings ▶ Place timber hollow edge down
Uneven finish	▶ Dull cutters causing 'chatter' marks on the timber	▶ Reverse/replace cutters ▶ Feed timber into the cutters at the correct rate
Pronounced cutter mark pattern	▶ Too fast feed rate	▶ Reduce feed rate
Timber 'drops' at the end of the cut and gouges out the end of the timber	▶ Outfeed table is too low	▶ Adjust outfeed table level with cutting circle
Excessive vibration causing a poor finish	▶ Worn bearings	▶ Renew bearings

Range of work

Function 2
To reduce, to the desired width and thickness, timber that has been previously faced and edged.

Parts of the Machine

Anti-kickback fingers
These reduce the chances of timber ejection or 'kickback' (Fig 4.17).

Infeed roller
This is fluted to grip the timber (Fig 4.17).

Chip breaker and pressure bar
Its function is to hold down the timber on the table prior to cutting, also to act as a chip breaker which prevents 'riving' of the grain and excessive splitting of the timber (Fig 4.17).

Outfeed pressure bar
Its function is to hold down the timber on the table to prevent the timber 'lifting' or 'chattering' (Fig 4.17).

Outfeed roller
The outfeed roller has a smooth surface to prevent marking on the planed surface (Fig 4.17).

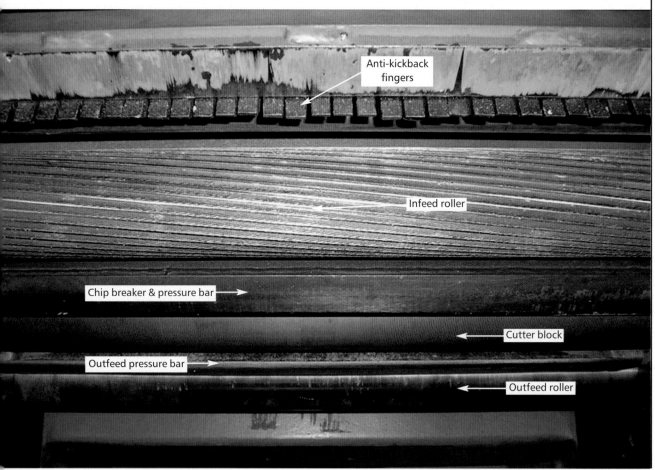

Fig 4.17

The infeed and outfeed rollers are power fed. The feed speed is variable from 6 to 18 m/min. This gives the desired surface finish, usually described as the cutter mark pitch (Fig 4.18). The rotation of the feed rollers is controlled by the direction switch (Fig 4.20).

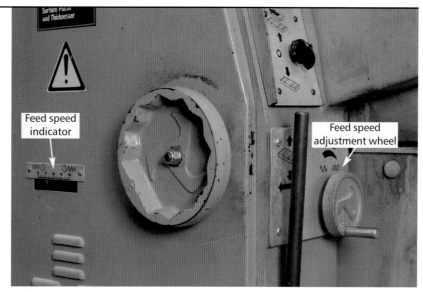

Fig 4.18

Antifriction rollers

These are placed under the infeed and outfeed rollers and are not power fed. They can be adjusted for height above the table, reducing the friction between the timber and the table (Fig 4.19).

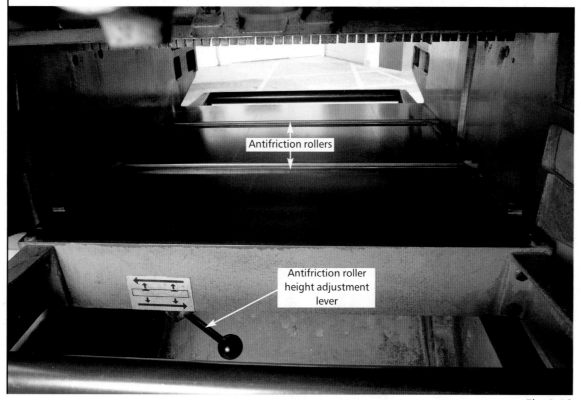

Fig 4.19

Rise and fall of thicknessing table

There are two methods of making this adjustment:

1. 'Powered' rise and fall: by use of the lever (a quick method of moving the table to the approximate required thickness). The speed of the adjustment is linked to the feed speed (faster feed equals faster rise and fall) and direction dictated by the direction switch (Fig 4.20).

2. 'Manual' rise and fall: by use of the wheel (slow movement to accurately position the table to the required thickness) (Fig 4.20).

There is a mechanical readout thicknessing scale in full view of the operator when carrying out the above adjustments (Fig 4.20).

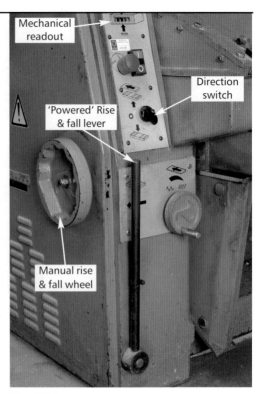

Fig 4.20

Controls

Stop/start buttons, brake

These must operate efficiently and be within easy reach of the operator. The additional stop button has a 'mushroom head' and a pull-to-release mechanism. The start button is shrouded to prevent accidental starting (Fig 4.21). To reduce the risk of contact with the cutter block during 'run down'.

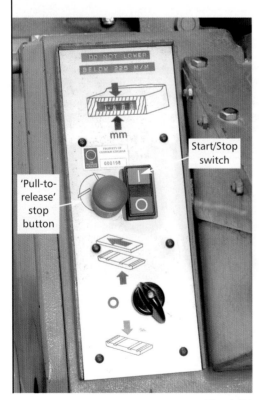

Fig 4.21

Machines should be fitted with a braking device that brings the blade to rest within 10 seconds.

The braking device is manually operated which also actuates the stop button, but it does not put the stop button in the locked position (Fig 4.14).

Jigs

Jigs are made by the machinist to enable certain operational cuts to be carried out safely. They must be of substantial construction, be safe to use and not endanger the operative using the jig.

Bevel jig

These are for bevelling lengths of timber (Fig 4.22) (antifriction rollers should be set to minimum height).

Fig 4.22

Fault diagnosis

Table 4.2 lists the more common faults which may occur when thicknessing timber.

Table 4.2

Fault	Cause	Remedy
Timber chopped at the beginning of thicknessing	▶ Bottom roller too high ▶ Chip breaker not working	▶ Reset bottom rollers ▶ Reset position of chip breaker
Timber chopped at the end of thicknessing	▶ Bottom rollers too high	▶ Reset bottom rollers
Indentations in the upper (just planed) side of the timber	▶ Outfeed roller has debris and resin build-up	▶ Clean out feed roller

▶

Fault	Cause	Remedy
Indentations in the lower (pre-planed) side of the timber	▶ Antifriction roller/s has debris and resin build-up	▶ Clean antifriction roller/s
Both edges of a piece of timber are not square after thicknessing	▶ Timber not faced and edged square	▶ Check fence is square on the surface planer, re-face and edge timber
Feed rollers fail to pull/push timber through machine	▶ Feed roller clogged by debris and resin build-up	▶ Clean feed roller
Torn grain	▶ Planing up timber against grain ▶ Blades blunt	▶ Check direction of grain before machining ▶ Reverse/replace

Maintenance

Planer knife storage

Planer knives are supplied in protective packaging and should remain so until required.

Planer knife disposal

Knives should be wrapped in protective packaging and disposed of correctly (they are still dangerous even though blunt!).

Questions

1. What tasks can be carried out on the combination planer?

. . . .

. . . .

. . . .

. . . .

. . . .

. . . .

2. Under PUWER 1998 what is the maximum time allowed for the brake to stop the rotation of the cutter block?

. . . .

. . . .

. . . .

. . . .

Questions

3. The position of the outfeed table in relation to the cutting circle should be:

    . . . .

    . . . .

    . . . .

    . . . .

4. The guard which must be set as close as possible to the timber when facing and/or edging is:

    . . . .

    . . . .

    . . . .

    . . . .

5. When facing or edging the feed speed is controlled by:

    . . . .

    . . . .

    . . . .

    . . . .

6. The slots in the infeed and outfeed tables either side of the cutter block are there to:

    . . . .

    . . . .

    . . . .

    . . . .

7. A piece of timber that has been thicknessed has a cutter pitch of 10 cuts per 25 mm, how can this be increased to improve the finish?

    . . . .

    . . . .

    . . . .

    . . . .

8. There is a 'chop' at the end of a piece of timber that has been thicknessed. What has caused this?

    . . . .

    . . . .

    . . . .

    . . . .

    . . . . Questions . . . .

▶

Questions

9. There are indentations in the just planed side of a piece of timber that has been thicknessed. How can this be prevented for the next cut?

. . . .

. . . .

. . . .

. . . .

. . . .

. . . .

. . . .

10. The first piece of timber in a batch of 20 has been thicknessed but is out of square. What was the cause of this and how can the remainder of the timber be corrected.

. . . .

. . . .

. . . .

. . . .

. . . .

. . . .

11. There are indentations in the opposite side to the just planed side of a piece of timber that has been thicknessed. How can this be prevented for the next cut?

. . . .

. . . .

. . . .

. . . .

. . . .

. . . .

12. On cylindrical limited projection cutter blocks the maximum projection is:

. . . .

. . . .

. . . .

. . . .

. . . . Wood Machine Guide : Combination Planer . . . .

Questions

13. On a batch of 50 pieces of timber already planed up. How would you accurately form a 12° chamfer?

. . . .

. . . .

. . . .

. . . .

. . . .

. . . .

5

Narrow Band Saw

Range of work

Fig 5.1

The saw is used to cut timber-based materials, either to a line, straight or curved, as well as tenon and wedge work, irregular shapes and circular work (Fig 5.1).

Parts of the machine

Fig 5.2

Table

The table is usually set at 90° to the blade (Fig 5.2) or canted up to 35° (Fig 5.3) for carrying out bevelled cuts.

Fig 5.3

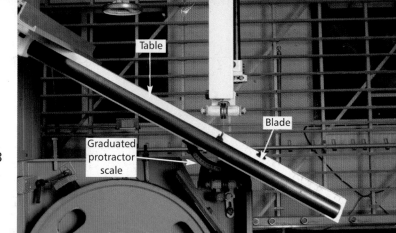

Fence

This is used to guide material when straight cutting.

The fence can be rotated to provide different heights (Figs 5.4 and 5.5).

Fence

Fig 5.4

Blade

It can be positioned on either side of the saw blade (Figs 5.5 and 5.6).

Fig 5.5

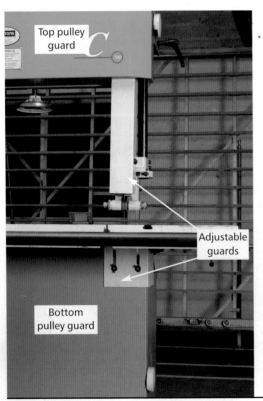

Top pulley guard

Adjustable guards

Bottom pulley guard

Fig 5.7

Fence adjustment & lock

Fig 5.6

Guarding

The pulleys and blade, except the part which runs downwards between the top pulley and machine table, are enclosed by substantial guards. An adjustable guard is provided to cover the blade between the table and top pulley (Fig 5.7). The guard is attached to, and moves with, the top blade guide. It should be adjusted as close to the material being cut as possible. A second adjustable guard is provided under the table between it and the bottom pulley guard and must be adjusted to guard the guide and blade at all times (Fig 5.7).

Pulley wheels and brushes:

Brushes are provided and adjusted so that they 'brush' away any sawdust that may become attached to the pulley wheels and blade (Figs 5.8 and 5.9). This prevents any unevenness or variation in the tension on the blade which may cause it to snap.

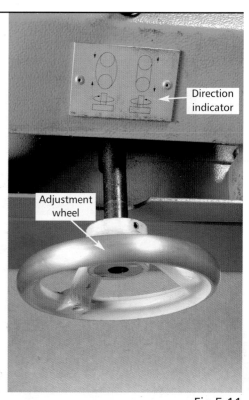

Fig 5.8

Fig 5.9

Tensioning

Tensioning is achieved by rotating the adjustment wheel (Figs 5.10 and 5.11) in the direction shown on the direction indicator (Fig 5.11) until the desired tension is indicated on the tension scale (Fig 5.10).

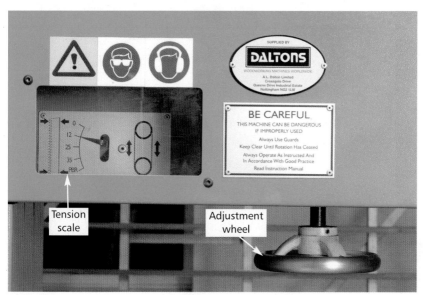

Fig 5.10

Fig 5.11

Tracking

Saw blades have different operating characteristics owing to the quality of ribbon from which the blade is made, blade jointing and the tension applied. These factors are compensated for on the machine by having a tilt adjustment on the top wheel (Fig 5.12). This adjustment ensures that the blade runs centrally on the pulley wheels and passes between them in a straight line without any 'snaking' movement. Once the tracking is set it is locked in place.

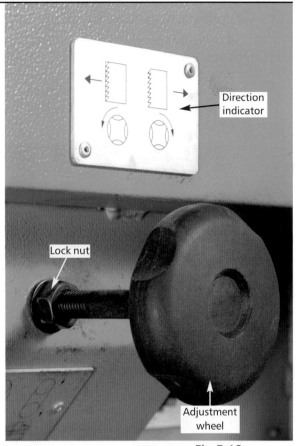

Fig 5.12

Blade guides and thrust wheels

These give support to the sides and rear of the blade when in use and are situated above the material being cut and below the machine table (Fig 5.13). These are set as close to the blade as possible and guide in line with the gullets of the saw blade (Fig 5.14).

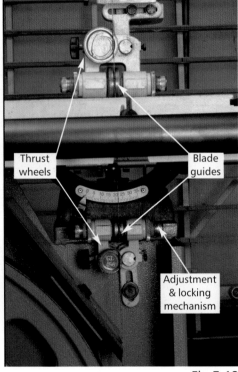

Fig 5.13

Fig 5.14

Square straight cutting

The fence (Fig 5.15) should be used whenever possible. However cuts not parallel to the edge may be cut 'freehand' following a line on the material (Fig 5.16).

Fig 5.15

Fig 5.16

Bevelled straight cutting

Bevel cutting is achieved by tilting the table. The cut can be carried out in conjunction with the fence (positioned on the right hand side of the blade, allowing gravity to assist holding the material against it) (Fig 5.17) or 'freehand' following a line on the material (Fig 5.18).

Fig 5.17

Fig 5.18

Curved cutting

Curved cuts are achieved by following a line marked on the material 'freehand' (Fig 5.19). Bevelled curved cuts can also be carried out.

Fig 5.19

Controls

Fig 5.20

Stop/start buttons, brake

These must operate efficiently and be within easy reach of the operator. The stop button has a 'mushroom head' and a twist to release mechanism. The start button is shrouded to prevent accidental starting (Fig 5.20). To reduce the risk of contact with the saw blade during 'run down', machines should be fitted with a braking device. The braking device is automatic and works in conjunction with the stop button.

> Machines must be fitted with a braking device that brings the blade to rest within 10 seconds.

Isolator

The function of the isolator is to cut off all power to the machine when setting up, changing tooling, carrying out maintenance or repairs. It should also be used when the machine is left unattended.
It can be 'pad locked' in the off position. A label can be attached when the blade is not tensioned (Fig 5.21).

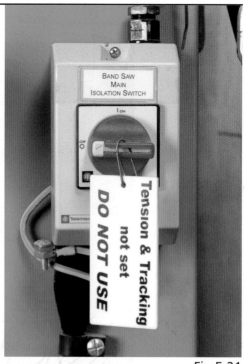

Fig 5.21

Cutout switches

The top and bottom pulley wheel guards have electronic sensors fitted to prevent machine start up when the guards are open (Fig 5.22).

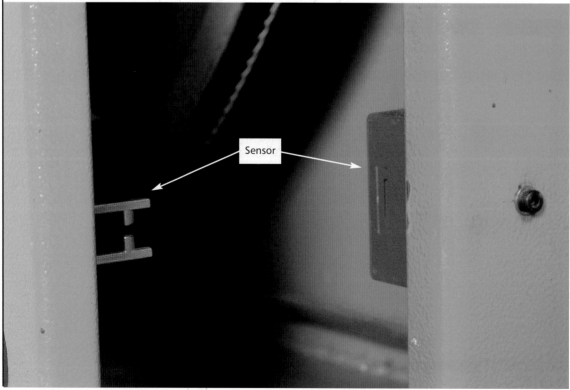

Fig 5.22

Jigs and stops

These are made by the machinist to enable certain operational cuts to be carried out safely. They must be of substantial construction, be safe to use and not endanger the operative using the jig.

Haunches or stopped cuts

Using jigs and stops ensures repetitive cutting of haunches on stopped cuts can be carried out safely and efficiently.

Fig 5.23 Fence and stop used for ripping down haunch

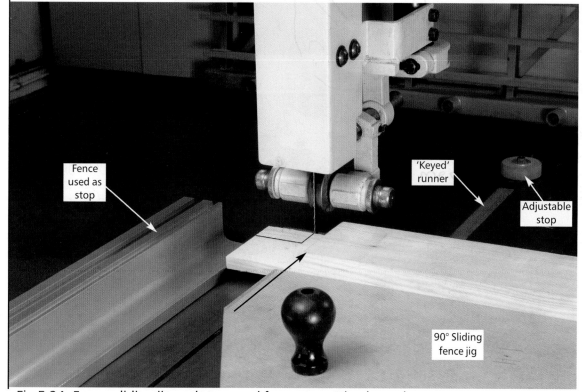

Fig 5.24 Fence, sliding jig and stop used for cross-cutting haunch

Wedges

A jig is used for safe, repetitive cutting of small wedges.

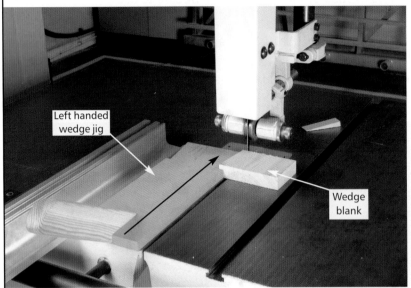

Fig 5.25

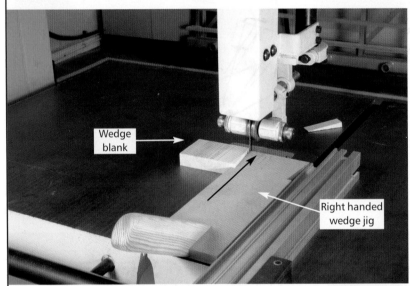

Fig 5.26

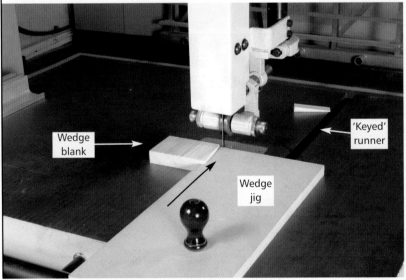

Fig 5.27

Once the wedge blank becomes small, a push stick (Fig 5.28) can be used to hold the blank in place. Wedge jigs can be used against the fence and be left handed (Fig 5.25), right handed (Fig 5.26) or use a 'keyed' runner in the machined groove in the machine table as a guide (Fig 5.27).

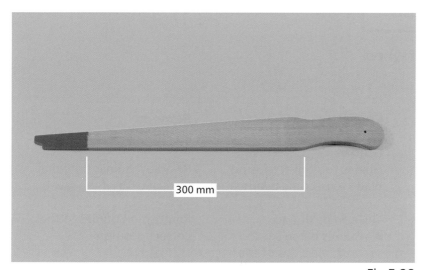

Fig 5.28

Circular work

A jig is required for cutting accurate circles, or segments of circles.

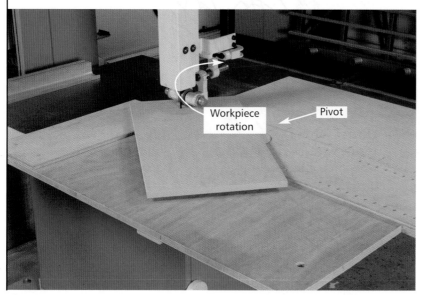

Workpiece
rotation

Pivot

Fig 5.29

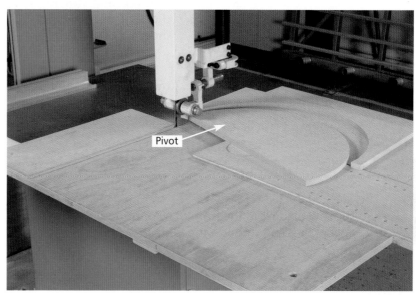

Pivot

Fig 5.30

Fault diagnosis

Saw guides and thrust wheel

Table 5.1

Fault	Cause	Remedy
	Guides	
Binding of the sides of the saw blade	Guides too tight, causing blade to become overheated	Re-adjust guides until they are just clear of the saw blade
Blade twists and deflects in the saw cut	This can be due to: ▶ Guides being set too far from the sides of the blade (not guiding blade) ▶ Guides are set too far back (not supporting the width of the blade)	Re-position guides to their correct position
Saw blade rubs on one side of the guide and the blade runs off line	Top guides above the table are not in line with guides below the table. This is due to: ▶ Incorrect adjustment for different widths of blade ▶ The saw running too far out of the guides ▶ Saw teeth contacting the guides	Re-align the guides with the running position of the blades by adjusting 'off centre' movement on the guides
	Thrust wheel	
Thrust wheel face is badly scored	Thrust wheel is not revolving when in contact with the blade due to: ▶ Lack of lubrication ▶ A worn bearing ▶ Incorrect positioning of the thrust wheel, i.e. the blade runs too near the centre of the wheel	▶ Apply lubricant as recommended in the instruction manual ▶ Replace thrust wheel ▶ Reposition thrust wheel so that the blade runs nearer to rim of thrust wheel
Thrust wheel runs hard against the back of the blade when it is not cutting	Incorrect adjustment of thrust wheel in relation to the back of saw blade	Reposition thrust wheel so that it just clears the blade
The thrust wheel is not contacting the back of the saw blade when cutting	Incorrect adjustment of thrust wheel in relation to the back of the saw blade	Reposition thrust wheel so that it just clears the blade

Saw blades

The saw blade is in the form of a continuous narrow strip running over two pulleys, passing through the table.

Inspect for width

To suit the radius of cut, narrow blades are used for small radii and light cutting. Wider blades are used for larger radii and heavier cutting.

Wheel diameter on Wadkin C700 = 700 mm
Maximum width of blade = 40 mm

To determine the length of a bandsaw blade length for any machine, the following formula is used:

Circumference = $\pi \times$ diameter
Length of blade = $2 \times$ distance between centres (DBC).

Therefore $2 \times$ DBC + Circumference of one wheel less 25 mm from the maximum length or plus 25 mm to the minimum length, allowing for straining.

Blade size minimum cutting radius

The width and thickness of the blade directly affects the radius that can be cut.

Table 5.2

Blade width in millimetres	Blade thickness in millimetres	Minimum cutting radius in millimetres
6	0.70	20
10	0.70	45
12.5	0.80	55
16	0.80	75
20	0.80	100
25	0.80	180
32	0.80	260
40	0.80	380

Blade condition

Check to see that it is:

▶ Sharp
▶ Correctly set
▶ Free from twists
▶ Free from cracks in the toothed or back edge
▶ Check that the brazed or welded joint is in good condition by flexing it gently to about 300 mm radius

Tooth shape

Various tooth shapes are available for cutting different materials:

▶ Skip tooth – plastics and timber
▶ Fine teeth – metals and denser plastics

▶ Standard teeth 5 degree Rake angle – softwood

▶ Standard teeth 5 degree Rake angle – hardwood

Length of blades

Minimum length = 4902 mm

Maximum length = 5080 mm

Standard saw teeth

Table 5.3

Width of blade mm	Pitch (P)mm
6	4.00
10	4.00 to 5.00
12.5	5.00 to 6.30
16	5.60 to 7.10
25	7.10 to 8.00
32	7.10 to 12.50
40	8.00 to 12.50

Fault diagnosis

Saw blades

Table 5.4

Faults	Cause	Remedy
Bandsaw breakages	▶ Badly brazed or butt welded joint ▶ Cracked saw blade ▶ Sharp square corner in the gullet of a tooth, causing a crack to form ▶ Twisting of the blade in the cut ▶ Incorrect setting of the guides and thrust wheel, i.e. guides bind on the thrust wheel ▶ Offcuts wedged between the blade and workpiece ▶ The saw buckles, due to forcing wood against the blade too fast	▶ Cut out the bad joint and re-braze or re-weld ▶ Re-joint blade ▶ Use the correct type of file ▶ Use a narrow blade for small radius work ▶ Re-adjust the guides and thrust wheel to suit blade position ▶ Renew mouthpiece regularly ▶ Use wider saw blade for heavy cuts, reduce feed rate

Saw blade runs off the wheel	▶ Incorrect tracking of blade ▶ Resin build up on the wheel, causing extra tension on the saw blade	▶ Re-track blade correctly ▶ Renew or re-adjust cleaning brush
Badly sawn finish	▶ Uneven set ▶ Buckled saw blade ▶ Uneven sharpening, all saw teeth not working ▶ Burning on the saw surface	▶ Re-set accurately ▶ Re-new blade ▶ Re-sharpen accurately ▶ Not enough set, re-set ▶ Blade too wide for radius of cut – change blade ▶ Feed speed too slow – causing blunting

Maintenance

Cleaning off resin deposits

There are several systems for cleaning resin deposits (all requiring the blade to be removed) using a tank or tray with a resin solvent, which do the job effectively. However, the most common method is the use of paraffin or white spirit. Brushed on then scraped off with a scraper made from timber. Do not forget to clean out the gullets.

Examining the saw teeth for cracks

Cracks, when they occur are usually in the gullet area, in line with the face of the tooth and are generally the result of incorrect filing giving a sharp corner in the gullet, or overheating at the base of the gullet when using a grinding wheel for gulleting.

Cracks are not always obvious to the naked eye. If one is suspected, a method of identification is to apply paraffin, wipe off the surplus with a rag, then apply French chalk powder over the saw. Leave for a period, wipe off the chalk, then a black line highlighting the crack should be visible.

Storage of the saw blades

Where the saw blade is being removed from the machine, to be replaced by a different blade, they need to be stored. They may be stored 'looped' into three (Fig 5.31) and laid flat on plywood shelves (Fig 5.32) to prevent damage to teeth and joint.

Fig 5.32

Fig 5.31

Questions

1. What tasks can be carried out on the narrow band saw?

    . . . .

    . . . .

    . . . .

    . . . .

    . . . .

    . . . .

2. What should the operator ensure before setting up the bandsaw?

    . . . .

    . . . .

    . . . .

    . . . .

    . . . .

    . . . .

3. Why is the thrust wheel positioned behind the blade?

    . . . .

    . . . .

    . . . .

    . . . .

    . . . .

    . . . .

4. Why is there provision for top pulley wheel vertical adjustment?

    . . . .

    . . . .

    . . . .

    . . . .

    . . . .

    . . . .

5. Why is there provision for top pulley wheel tilt adjustment?

    . . . .

    . . . .

    . . . .

    . . . .

    . . . .

    . . . .

Questions

6. Why are saw guides positioned on either side of the blade?

   . . . .

   . . . .

   . . . .

   . . . .

   . . . .

   . . . .

7. What is the maximum run down time allowed after depressing the stop button?

   . . . .

   . . . .

   . . . .

   . . . .

8. The teeth on a blade must face which direction at table height?

   . . . .

   . . . .

   . . . .

9. The minimum diameter of a circle that can be cut is directly related to what?

   . . . .

   . . . .

   . . . .

10. Where should the upper adjustable guard be positioned?

    . . . .

    . . . .

    . . . .

    . . . .

    . . . .

    . . . .

11. A narrow bandsaw blade must be stored correctly to prevent what?

    . . . .

    . . . .

    . . . .

    . . . .

    . . . .

    . . . .

Questions

12. Why is it necessary to remove the tension form the blade overnight or when not in use for long periods?

....

....

....

....

....

....

13. How would a large number of wedges be manufactured on the narrow bandsaw?

....

....

....

....

....

....

14. How should you leave the machine on completing a task?

....

....

....

....

....

....

6

Morticer

This is a combined chisel and chain mortice machine. It is capable of accurately cutting mortice holes. For clarity there are two sections: first, the chisel morticer and second, the chain morticer.

Fig 6.1

Chisel morticer

Range of work

The chisel morticer is used for accurately cutting mortice holes of various widths and depths.

Parts of the machine

Carriage

The machine can be adjusted in three directions (Fig 6.2):

1. Sideways is operated by a hand wheel which moves the carriage by means of a rack and pinion.

2. Forward/Backward is operated by a hand wheel and screw mechanism.

3. Rise and Fall is operated by a hand wheel gearing through a spiral which turns a large screw.

Fig 6.2

Headstock

The headstock is positioned by use of the re-set collar to give the shortest working stroke that is practicable (Fig 6.3).

Double depth stops

These are provided to enable two predetermined depths (Fig 6.3). The top collar is for haunches. The bottom collar is for stub mortices and the first cut of 'through' mortices.

Operating handle position and leverage

The handle should be adjusted to give good leverage, control and comfortable swing (Fig 6.3). The handle release nut disengages/ engages teeth on the lever and casting for adjustment.

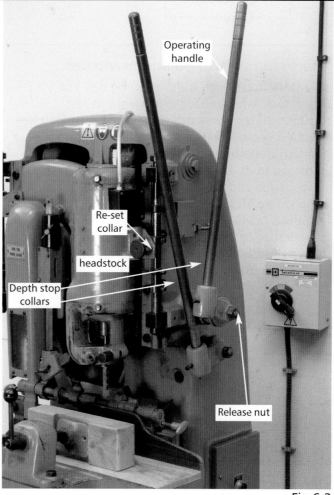

Operating handle

Re-set collar

headstock

Depth stop collars

Release nut

Fig 6.3

Carriage clamp

This clamp holds the material being morticed securely (Fig 6.4). The locking mechanism can be released by means of a lever to allow rapid adjustment across the carriage. The clamp bar locks and pressure is applied. A hardwood/softwood buffer piece is positioned between the face of the clamp and the timber being machined to prevent marking.

Fig 6.4

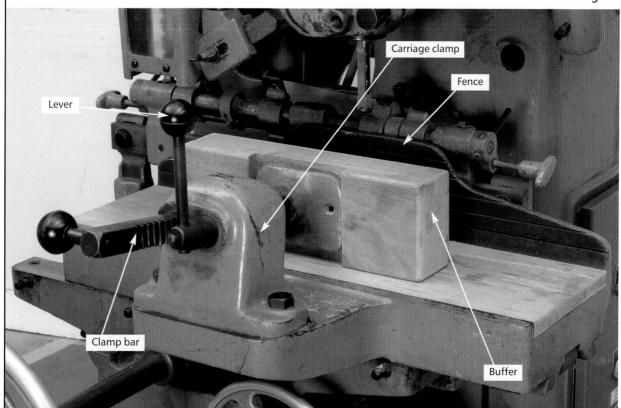

Carriage clamp

Fence

Lever

Clamp bar

Buffer

Controls

Start/stop switch, isolation switches

The start/stop switch is shown in Fig 6.5. The headstock, when moved down from its rest position allows the depth stop bar with an attached switch lever to lower and operate the 'spring loaded' start/stop switch. When the headstock is returned to its rest position, the start/stop switch is disengaged and the machine comes to a complete stop within 10 seconds and therefore does not require a brake. The switch can be made inoperative by locking the depth stop bar in the raised position by means of a locking handle (the machine must be isolated before any adjustments are made).

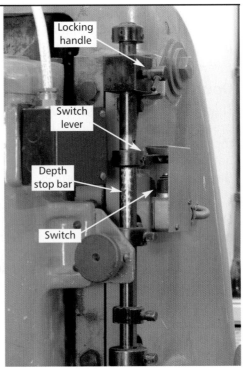

Fig 6.5

Isolator switches

There are two isolator switches for this machine. One is situated on the machine itself (Fig 6.6), on the right hand side towards the bottom of the main casing. The other is on the wall behind the machine (Fig 6.7) which can be 'locked off'. The one on the wall conforms to the current electrical health and safety requirements.

Fig 6.6

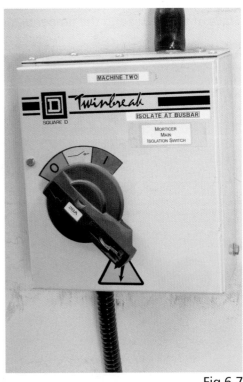

Fig 6.7

Chisel, auger, bushes, etc.

This consists of a hollow square chisel, which has a hole lengthways through its centre and windows in the side (Fig 6.8). The chisel is set in the machine with one end directed at the timber to be morticed. The four inside faces of this end are formed into cutting edges. Inside the chisel runs an auger (similar to a 'Jennings' twist bit but without a screw or brad point). The chisel cuts the sides of the mortice and the

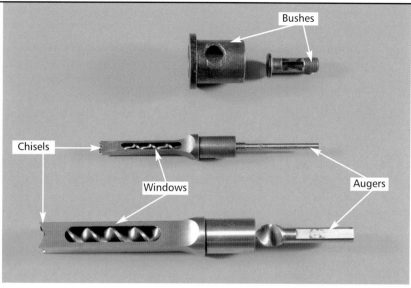

Fig 6.8

auger removes the material from within the chisel, which is then ejected through the windows, which are positioned inline with the mortice hole to reduce clogging. Bushes are used to allow chisels and augers of various sizes to fit into the machine (Fig 6.8). However the larger auger and chisel combinations may not require a bush or bushes.

Fault diagnosis

Table 6.1 lists the more common faults, possible cause and remedy.

Table 6.1

Fault	Possible cause	Remedy
Cuts out of square	▶ Chisel not square with fence	▶ Square chisel with fence
Uneven bottom	▶ Auger too far in advance of the chisel	▶ Reposition the auger

▶

Fault	Possible cause	Remedy
Chipping build up inside chisel	▶ Bad clearance, auger spiral does not extend far enough, or resinous timber 'gumming-up' inside of chisel	▶ Remove auger and clean with paraffin periodically
chisel becomes hot near centre when working		
Blued and cracked	▶ Bent auger	▶ Straighten/replace auger
	▶ Auger rubbing against chisel edge causing overheating	▶ Reposition auger, regrind/replace chisel

Chain Morticer

Range of work

The chain morticer is used for accurately cutting mortice holes of various widths and depths.

Parts of the Machine

Carriage

The carriage can be adjusted in three directions (Fig 6.14):

1. Sideways is operated by a hand wheel which moves the carriage by means of a rack and pinion.

2. Forward/Backward is operated by a hand wheel and screw mechanism.

3. Rise and Fall is operated by a hand wheel gearing through a spiral which turns a large screw.

Fig 6.14

Headstock

This is positioned by the use of the re-set collar to give the shortest working stroke practicable (Fig 6.15).

Double depth stops

These are provided to enable two predetermined depths (Fig 6.15). The top collar is for haunches. The bottom collar is for stubs and the first cut of 'through' mortices.

Operating handle position and leverage:

The handle should be adjusted to give good leverage, control and comfortable swing (Fig 6.16). The handle release nut disengages/engages teeth on the lever and casting for adjustment.

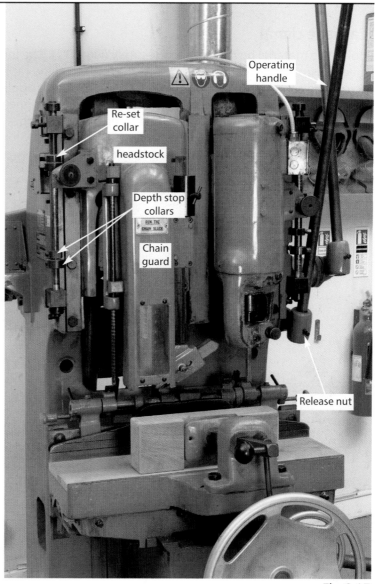

Re-set collar

headstock

Depth stop collars

Chain guard

Operating handle

Release nut

Fig 6.15

Fig 6.16

Carriage clamp

Holds the material being morticed securely (Fig 6.17). The locking mechanism can be released by means of a lever to allow rapid adjustment across the carriage. The clamp bar locks and pressure is applied. A hardwood/softwood buffer piece is positioned between the face of the clamp and the timber being machined to prevent marking.

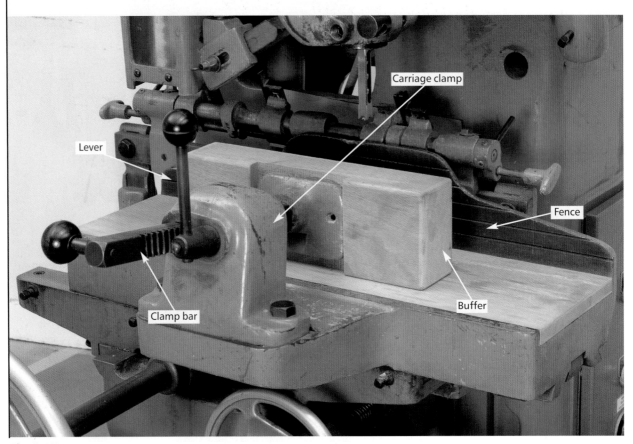

Fig 6.17

Controls

Start/stop switch, isolation switches

The start/stop switch is shown in Fig 6.18. The headstock, when moved down from its rest position allows the depth stop bar with the attached switch lever to lower and operate the 'spring loaded' start/stop switch. When the headstock is retuned to its rest position, the start/stop switch is disengaged and the machine comes to a complete stop within 10 seconds and therefore does not require a brake. The switch can be made inoperative by locking the depth stop bar in the raised position by means of a locking handle (the machine must be isolated before any adjustments are made).

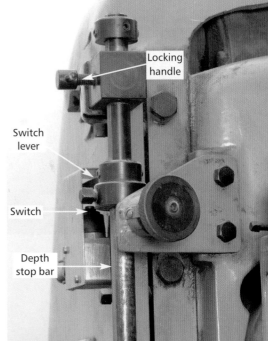

Fig 6.18

Isolator switches

There are two isolator switches for this machine. One is situated on the machine itself (Fig 6.19), on the right hand side towards the bottom of the main casting. The other is on the wall behind the machine (Fig 6.20), which can be 'locked off'. The one on the wall conforms to the current electrical health and safety requirements.

Fig 6.19

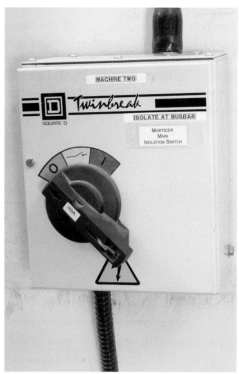

Fig 6.20

Chain, guide bar and drive sprocket

This consists of an endless chain fitted with teeth (Fig 6.20). The chain is set in the machine with one end directed at the timber to be morticed. The chain is driven by the drive sprocket and guided by the guide bar (Fig 6.20). The chain cuts a slot in the timber and the waste is ejected by the motion of the chain. The chain cuts on both the downward and upward motion.

Fig 6.21

Therefore a chip breaker (Fig 6.22) is positioned to help prevent the timber spelching on the upward cut of the chain. Various widths of chain are available to provide a selection of mortice widths.

The chain is driven by the drive sprocket, tension is set by means of the tension screw, the guide bar is held in position by the securing nut and the chip breaker is positioned against the upward running side of the chain. The chip breaker is held against the timber during machining by the chip breaker weight to help prevent the timber spelching. The chain is enclosed by the chain guard during operation.

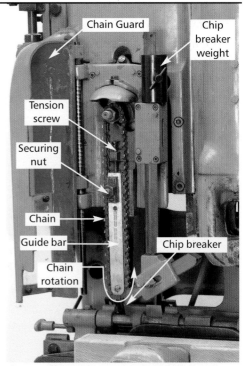

Fig 6.22

Fault diagnosis

Table 6.2 lists the more common faults, possible cause and remedy

Table 6.2

Fault	Possible cause	Remedy
Timber spelches on the upward cut of the chain	▶ End of chipbreaker badly worn ▶ End of chipbreaker – incorrect angle cut on end	▶ Replace/re-cut end of chipbreaker
Bottom of mortice hole is elongated	▶ Chain is running too slack	▶ Re-tension chain

Questions

1. What tasks can be carried out on the morticing machine?

   ....
   ....
   ....
   ....
   ....
   ....

2. Why does this machine not require a brake to comply with PUWER 1998?

   ....
   ....
   ....
   ....
   ....
   ....

3. Why must the carriage not be moved when the chisel/auger is in the timber?

   ....
   ....
   ....
   ....
   ....
   ....

4. Before adjusting any part of the machine what must be done?

   ....
   ....
   ....
   ....
   ....
   ....

5. How is the motor to the auger or chain started?

   ....
   ....
   ....
   ....
   ....

Questions

6. State one cause of the chisel overheating and turning blue?

    . . . .

    . . . .

    . . . .

7. The bottom of a stub mortice has clearly defined circular holes. How may this be prevented?

    . . . .

    . . . .

    . . . .

    . . . .

    . . . .

    . . . .

8. A mortice hole has a series of vertical grooves on each side. What was the cause?

    . . . .

    . . . .

    . . . .

    . . . .

    . . . .

    . . . .

9. When setting up the chisel where should the window(s) be positioned?

    . . . .

    . . . .

    . . . .

    . . . .

    . . . .

10. In accordance with current legislation, what must the person setting up and/or operating the machine be?

    . . . .

    . . . .

    . . . .

    . . . .

    . . . .

    . . . .

Questions

11. Why must the chip breaker be held against the timber during machining?

   . . . .

   . . . .

   . . . .

   . . . .

   . . . .

   . . . .

Information point

General

Safe working at woodworking machines PDF – woodworking information sheet 15 (31 kb)
http://www.hse.gov.uk/pubns/wis15.pdf

PUWER 98: Selection of tooling for use with hand-fed woodworking machines PDF –
woodworking information sheet 37
http://www.hse.gov.uk/pubns/wis37.pdf

Safe use of woodworking machinery – Provision and Use of Work Equipment Regulations
1998 as applied to woodworking machinery – Approved Code of Practice and Guidance –
L114

Simple guide to the Provision and Use of Work Equipment Regulations 1998
http://www.hse.gov.uk/pubns/indg291.pdf

Health and Safety Executive
http://www.hse.gov.uk

Specific

Radial arm saw

Safe use of manually operated cross cut saws PDF – woodworking information sheet 36
http://www.hse.gov.uk/pubns/wis36.pdf

Dimension saw

Circular saw benches: safe working practices PDF – woodworking information sheet 16
http://www.hse.gov.uk/pubns/wis16.pdf

Surface planer and Combination planers

Safe use of hand-fed planing machines PDF – woodworking information sheet 17
http://www.hse.gov.uk/pubns/wis17.pdf

Narrow bandsaw

Safety in the use of narrow band saws – woodworking information sheet 31
http://www.hse.gov.uk/pubns/wis31.htm

Glossary

Anti-friction rollers
Rollers positioned in the table to reduce the effects of friction.

Anti-kickback fingers
Device to prevent the material being ejected.

Blade guides
Gives support to the sides of the bandsaw blade when in use.

Bow
Warp along length of material.

Brake
Stops moving parts of the machine in accordance with current legislation.

Bridge Guard
Adjustable part of the machine designed to reduce exposure of the cutter block.

Brushes
Adjustable, 'fixed' to the bandsaw to remove or 'brush' away sawdust that may become attached to the pulley wheels.

Canting
The ability to tilt the saw blade, table or fence up to 45°.

Carriage
Part of the morticing machine for supporting and positioning material when morticing.

Carriage clamp
Holds the material securely to the carriage.

Chip breaker
Applies light pressure to the material in front of the cutter to reduce 'chatter' and splitting.

Clearance angle
Space behind the cutting edge.

Compound cut
A cut that consists of both vertical and horizontal angles.

Cross-cutting
Cut material (timber) across the grain.

Crown guard
Guards the top portion of the saw blade.

Cup
Warp across width of material.

Cutter block
Part of the machine that houses the cutters.

Cutter knife/planer knife
Precision-ground blade.

Deeping
Cutting to thickness (through the wide section).

Depth stop
Controls the depth at which tooling can penetrate materials.

Distancing aid
Device used to distance the operator from dangerous parts of the machine.

Extension piece
Adjustable guard attached to the crown guard.

Extension table
Placed behind the saw table to comply with current legislation; acts as a distancing aid.

Fence
Precision-ground surface adjacent to table.

Flatting
Cutting to width (through narrowest section).

Guard
Reduces exposure of the moving parts of a machine.

Gullet
Space between roots of the tooth.

Hook
Angle of the teeth on a saw blade (can range from positive to negative).

Infeed roller
Grips and feeds the material towards the tooling.

Infeed table
Table positioned before the cutter block on a surface planer.

Isolator
Isolates machine from power supply.

Jig
Device used to distance/support/guide the material to enable non-standard and/or repetitive machine operations.

Kerf
Width of cut made by the saw 'blade'.

Mitring
Any angle cut on a timber section (normally 45°).

Outfeed roller
Grips and feeds the material away from the tooling.

Outfeed table
Table positioned after the cutter block on a surface planer.

Pitch
Number of occurrences in a set distance.

Pressure bar
Applies light pressure to the material behind the cutter.

Pulley wheel
Wheel to support and drive the bandsaw blade.

Range of work
What the machine is capable of carrying out safely, while adhering to current legislation.

Resin
A substance contained within timber.

Rise and fall mechanism
Device to raise and lower parts of the machine and or tooling.

Riving knife
Device positioned to reduce material binding on the circular saw blade.

Roller table
Gives support and manoeuverablity to materials being cut.

Root
Base of tooth.

Shaw guard
Adjustable auxiliary guard attached to the machine that applies pressure both horizontally and vertically on the material being machined.

Start/stop buttons
Buttons that start the motor at the beginning of an operation and stop it at the end.

Stops
Allow accurate repetitive cutting to length/width of timber-based materials.

Table lip
Edge of table closest to cutter block.

Table/machine bed
Precision-ground surface to support material.

Tensioning (1)
Tightening of the bandsaw blade.

Tensioning (2)
A method of inducing tension within a saw blade plate, so that it runs 'true' when 'hot' in use.

Tersa
Make of cutter block which has disposable cutter knifes.

Thrust wheel
Gives support to the back of the bandsaw blade when in use.

Tooling
Performs the cutting operation.

Tracking
Correctly positioning bandsaw blade on pulley wheels.

Tungsten carbide tip
Hard tip brazed to each tooth of the saw blade.